THEN & NOW®

MISSOULA

Opposite: This 1895 photograph shows a muddy Higgins Avenue at the intersection of Main Street. It is similar to the photograph on page 11 but from a different angle. The building on the right is the First National Bank, built in 1890 with a wooden sidewalk along its side. All the buildings on the left have been replaced since the photograph was taken. Not many downtown images from before 1900 are available. (University of Montana–Missoula, No. 78-15.)

MISSOULA

Philip Maechling
and Stan Cohen

Copyright © 2010 by Philip Maechling and Stan Cohen
ISBN 978-0-7385-8078-4

Library of Congress Control Number: 2009943320

Published by Arcadia Publishing
Charleston, South Carolina

Printed in the United States of America

Then and Now is a registered trademark and is used under license from
Salamander Books Limited

For all general information contact Arcadia Publishing at:
Telephone 843-853-2070
Fax 843-853-0044
E-mail sales@arcadiapublishing.com
For customer service and orders:
Toll-Free 1-888-313-2665

Visit us on the Internet at www.arcadiapublishing.com

ON THE FRONT COVER: The intersection of Cedar Street (now Broadway) and Higgins Avenue has always been one of Missoula's busiest locales. The surroundings (including the dirt roads and wooden sidewalks) have changed drastically, as seen in these 1894 and modern views, but not the bustling populace. For more on this topic, see page 14. (Then, Pictorial Histories Publishing Company; now, Philip Maechling.)

ON THE BACK COVER: This archway was constructed across Higgins Avenue for the Fraternal Order of Eagles state convention, held in Missoula from July 21 to 23, 1908. The local aerie was established on October 22, 1899, with 54 charter members. The Donohue Building in the background was a major department store in the downtown area and was replaced by a new Montgomery Ward store in the mid-1930s. It is now the location of the First Montana Bank. (Pictorial Histories Publishing Company.)

CONTENTS

ACKNOWLEDGMENTS

Historic images in this book were obtained from archives in Missoula and Helena. A number of them came from the K. Ross Toole Archives at the Mansfield Library at the University of Montana–Missoula, courtesy of Donna McCrea and Mark Fritch, and from the Montana Historical Society in Helena. The university images are marked "UM," and the society's are marked "MHS." The greatest number of historic images are from the archives of coauthor Stan Cohen and his publishing business, Pictorial Histories Publishing Company, marked "PHPC." Other historical images are acknowledged as to their source.

Modern images were taken by the two authors and university intern Ross Carlson, all in 2009. In addition, the authors would like to thank the following for providing photographs, information, or for posing for modern photographs: Kristie Hager, Marcie James, Chris Autio, Kermit Edmonds, Rachel Bartlett, Carolyn Thompson, Dennis Sain, Bill and Jan Taylor, Kris Crawford, Hayes Otopoulik, the American Legion Post Honor Guard, Libby Langston, the U.S. Forest Service archives, and Carol Guthrie of the Nine Mile area. Others to be thanked are the Missoula Office of Planning and Grants, Erik Benson, and Jody Allison-Bunnel, who coproduced the original Missoula Then and Now project with Philip Maechling.

INTRODUCTION

Missoula has been known as "The River City," "The Garden City," and the "Hub of Five Valleys." Whatever it is called, it has become the second-largest city in the state and the oldest major city in the state.

Its beginning was in 1860 with the establishment of Hellgate Village about 4 miles west of downtown on the old Mullan Military Road. A trading post was established by Francis Worden and C. P. Higgins to serve miners, traders, and Native Americans. Several outlaws were hung at Hellgate by an organized vigilante group. In 1864, a water-powered mill was built in the present downtown area by the Missoula (Clark Fork) River, and the town has grown steadily since then.

With the arrival of the Northern Pacific Railway in 1883, the town became a railroad center. From that date into the early 1900s, many large buildings spread out to the south in the downtown area, and hotels were built near the railroad stations to serve passengers. A second railway, the Milwaukee Road, came to the south side of Missoula in 1910.

A first bridge was built across the river, continuing Higgins Avenue to the south in the 1870s. The university was established south of the river in 1898, and the entire area started to expand from there.

The Western Montana Fair was started in 1879 and moved to its present site in 1915. In 1877, citizens asked for military protection from some Native American tribes, and Fort Missoula was established. More than 1,000 Italian seamen were interned at the fort from 1941 until 1944. After the Pearl Harbor attack, hundreds of Japanese Americans were sent to the fort from their homes on the West Coast.

The U.S. Forest Service established its first regional office in Missoula in 1905, and the timber industry greatly expanded in the early 20th century, including the mills in the Bonner area east of town. Sugar beets were a big crop at one time, and ranching is still important to Missoula's economy.

Today the city of Missoula has nearly 70,000 residents and is the trading, medical, governmental, educational, and recreational center for western Montana and nearby Idaho. There is a very active historic preservation presence with the Missoula Historic Preservation Commission and the nonprofit Preserve Historic Missoula. Nine historic districts have been established in the city, and there are more than 70 sites and districts listed on the National Register of Historic Places in Missoula County.

The authors of this book have tried to pick most of the most historic buildings and sites in the city and outlying areas, with some of the photographs published here for the first time. As with other cities in the country, progress has changed the look of Missoula, and it is a constant battle to preserve the city's heritage. Most of the "now" images have been taken as close as possible to the sites of the "then" images.

CHAPTER 1

STREETSCAPES

This very detailed photograph was taken in 1894 at the corner of Higgins Avenue and Main Street at a different angle than the photograph on page 3. The streets were dirt until paved with brick in 1912. The Chicago Bee Hive was founded in 1883 in Chicago as a popular store devoted to selling low-priced merchandise. On the far left is a horse-drawn streetcar; the service was electrified in 1910. The large building was attached to the original 1888 Florence Hotel, which burned down in 1913. All of these buildings have been replaced through the years. (UM.)

North Higgins Avenue is pictured here, possibly around 1905, as every vehicle appears to be horse-drawn. The west side of Higgins Avenue is shown in the block connected to Cedar (later Broadway) Street. This is some type of patriotic parade or perhaps a historical pageant. The military band would be from Fort Missoula. Most of these buildings have been replaced through the years. Streetcar tracks can be seen in the dirt street. (Then, PHPC via Bob VanGieson; now, Stan Cohen.)

This scene on East Front Street looking east was probably taken in the 1920s and would be either a Fourth of July or Memorial Day parade. The Missoula Mercantile building is on the left, with the Elks Club in the background. The First National Bank is on the right. Other than a new bank building, this scene looks similar today. (Then, PHPC via Bob VanGieson; now, Philip Maechling.)

This interesting 1911 photograph is of Cedar (Broadway) Street looking east. The Missoula Band is getting ready to load onto the Bonner streetcar, which was just electrified the year before. The Masonic Temple building in the background was opened in 1909 and was the headquarters of W. A. Clark's Missoula Light and Water Company. The building to the left was the Scandinavian-American Bank, which was designed by A. J. Gibson and used partially as his office. (Then, PHPC; now, Philip Maechling.)

This never-before-published photograph from 1912 shows bricks stacked up for the first brick paving of North Higgins Avenue. Looking south on the left is the old Belmont Hotel building, which is still in use. The Hotel Shapard, on the right, burned down in 1942, and the building on the far right is the Atlantic Hotel, which is still in use as a secondhand store and apartments. On the extreme left is an open field used for years as a baseball diamond and circus and carnival site. The Circle Square building now occupies this space. (Then, PHPC; now, Philip Maechling.)

A child races along the sidewalk on East Pine Street on June 24, 1923. Missoula's first residential neighborhood developed in the 1870s and 1880s as prominent citizens, including Francis Worden and Joseph Dixon, built their homes there. Worden imported maple trees for the boulevards. In 1915, Dixon petitioned the city to create green medians and tree-lined boulevards on East Pine in keeping with Missoula's image as the "Garden City." As cars and traffic have become primary considerations, the medians on East Pine Street have survived many challenges, as have many of the historic residences in the area. Retaining the medians slows traffic, helping the neighborhood retain its unique urban character instead of blending into the busy and treeless surrounding streets. The area became a National Register of Historic Places historic district in 1989. (Then, UM, No. 87-285, R. H. McKay Photographs, K. Ross Toole Archives; now, photograph by Kristi Hager.)

Main Street is pictured looking east in 1908. The cross street is Higgins Avenue. The Higgins Block is the domed building on the left. The other buildings on this side were replaced through the years. Buildings on the right side of the photograph have been restored in the past few years. The Chicago Bee Hive is at the corner, and the Union Block (Western Montana National Bank) is opposite. At this time, the *Daily Missoulian* was located on Main Street. The La Flesch Building on the right reflects the original Missoulian Building's design. (Then, PHPC; now, Philip Maechling.)

Higgins Avenue is pictured at Front Street looking north about 1925. Missoula had horse-drawn streetcars as early as 1890; the cars were electrified in 1910. Downtown streets, formerly rivers of alternating dust and mud, were paved with brick in 1912–1913. The second Florence Hotel, built in 1913 after the original 1888 building burned, appears on the left. The Missoula Mercantile Company's main building, constructed from 1874 to 1910 and housing one of Missoula's most important businesses, appears on the right. The streets are full of shoppers. Both continuity and change characterize this intersection. The second Florence Hotel burned in 1936 and was replaced by the present structure in 1941. It was a hotel until 1975, when it was remodeled into offices while leaving the exterior intact. Allied Stores purchased the Missoula Mercantile in 1959. It became the Bon Marche by 1970 and then Macy's in 2005 (now closed). Missoula's streetcar system took its last run in January 1932; smooth pavement replaced brick streets in the 1940s and 1960s. Area business owners responded to economic downturn in the 1970s by concentrating on revitalization and preservation. The downtown historic district remains a destination, and Missoula has received national recognition for preserving historic properties. (Then, UM, No. 90-463, Stan Healy photograph, K. Ross Toole Archives; now, photograph by Marcy James.)

East Front Street is seen from just west of Higgins Avenue around 1885. On the left is the Mercantile building before the second story was added to the easterly addition. Businesses on the right include the old Florence Laundry, farm implement sales, a saloon, and an opera house on the second floor of the building farthest to the right. Macy's, in the old Missoula Mercantile building, is in the oldest continuously occupied retail building in the Downtown Historic District. (Then, PHPC; now, Philip Maechling.)

Downtown Missoula, looking north from the Penwell Building at Higgins Avenue and Third Street, is seen in 1924. The Wilma Theater, to the left, had just been completed in 1920 as a theater with residences above and a swimming pool below. The First National Bank Building on the right was completed in 1891; just in front of it is the power plant that provided electricity and steam heat to many downtown buildings. Also visible are the first Central School, First Methodist Church, and the county hospital. Cars gliding across a wider bridge have replaced streetcars in this image. The Wilma is intact, but the First National Bank Building was razed in 1962, along with the old power plant. The Millennium Building, containing offices and residences, became part of the skyline in 2000. (Then, UM, No. 94-1516, R. H. McKay Photographs, K. Ross Toole Archives; now, photograph by Marcy James.)

Bicycles have always been evident in Missoula. This image from North Higgins Avenue in 1900 shows a bicycle shop on the left side, with a ramp from the dirt street to the plank sidewalk. On both sides of the street are a large variety of retail businesses, including bakeries, grocery stores, a harness shop, and even a secondhand store. Down Higgins Avenue is the landmark Higgins Block Building and the Dixon Block. The public library is on the second floor above a grocery store, where the Dana Gallery is now. (Then, courtesy UM; now, Philip Maechling.)

S TREETSCAPES

The Depression-era Farm Security Administration sent photographers all over the country in the 1930s and early 1940s to depict American life through photographs. This is one of two taken in 1942 of West Broadway and is of the 800 block looking east. Notice all the gas stations along the way and the price of gas at the time. The vehicle in the middle with the big headlights is one of the cars that the Gilmore Oil Company used to promote its products. Broadway Street is still one of the most important routes bisecting the city. (Then, Library of Congress; now, Philip Maechling.)

CHAPTER

FORT MISSOULA

This McKay photograph was taken about 1942. The rows of barracks were built to house more than 1,000 Italian detainees sent to the fort in early 1941. About 900 Japanese aliens and Japanese Americans from the West Coast were also sent to the fort right after the Pearl Harbor attack. Structures in the far upper left were CCC buildings along with the 1912 commissary building, which is now part of the 36-acre Historical Museum at Fort Missoula.

The base hospital is the large building close to the river. The water tower is in the lower left along with part of the Missoula Country Club's golf course. The large log recreation building in the upper middle was built by the CCC and burned down in 1946. The Northern Rockies Heritage Center owns the oval officer's row in the upper right along with several other buildings. In 2010, the army will vacate the entire fort. (PHPC.)

This is an idyllic setting for two young girls sitting on the original salute gun at Fort Missoula about 1917. The old officers' quarters can be seen in the background. The gun was a Civil War 1861 model 3-inch ordnance rifle converted to a breech-loading salute gun used from 1883 to 1942 for reveille and retreat. It was fired on the banks of the nearby Bitterroot River. Hayes and Amalia Otoupalik of Missoula donated the gun to the Historical Museum at Fort Missoula in 2008, and it is now on display in front of the main museum building. (Then, PHPC; now, Philip Maechling.)

In 1912, the old 1877 Fort Missoula was reconstructed with many new buildings to house regular army troops. This is officer's row, with mainly duplexes built for the officers of the 4th Infantry, which garrisoned the fort. After World War II, they were occupied by ROTC officers and others until being vacated in 2000. Then the Northern Rockies Heritage Center was established, and with some federal grants, it took over possession of these historic buildings and others to manage them and rent them out to nonprofit organizations. (Then, PHPC; now, Philip Maechling.)

Another row of officers' quarters was constructed at the same time on the parade grounds, along with two large two-story barracks buildings, one of which is shown in the background. The quarters were used for years after World War II to house professors at the university, but they were all torn down by the mid-1960s. The large barracks building to the right was headquarters for the U.S. Army Reserves for years. The adjacent barracks building is headquarters for the Lolo National Forest and Missoula Ranger District of the U.S. Forest Service. (Then, courtesy PHPC; now, Philip Maechling.)

Barracks buildings and foundations at Fort Missoula are pictured about 1941. The fort was established in 1877 at the request of area settlers who feared native attacks but served almost no military purpose until World War II. The U.S. Immigration and Naturalization Service then used it to house Italian prisoners of war and Japanese American internees. The rows of barracks on the right were constructed in 1941 to house those individuals. The fort was chosen for its remote inland location—and it was remote even from Missoula. Other buildings visible in this image were constructed about 1915. No active military units have been assigned to the fort since 1947. The barracks were mostly torn down in the 1950s, with a few moved to the Western Montana Fairgrounds for reuse. The fate of this large piece of land has been debated since before World War II, with a tug-of-war over whether it should be developed or retained as open space. In 1976, a year after the founding of the Historical Museum at Fort Missoula, the area was designated Missoula's first National Register of Historic Places historic district. In 2000, the fort was formally decommissioned, and control of the parade grounds and surrounding buildings passed to the Northern Rockies Heritage Center. Many of the historic structures—and the water tower from which this photograph was taken—remain intact. (Then, UM, No. 82-220, James Murray Papers, K. Ross Toole Archives; now, photograph by Chris Autio.)

Sometime in the 1930s, the army at Fort Missoula moved its target range from near the fort to its timber reserve in the Pattee Canyon area. Trees were cleared and berms placed at 100-yard intervals for soldiers to fire at targets, which can be seen in the far background. This area is now part of the U.S. Forest Service and is used as a recreation area. The berms and concrete boxes for the radio operators can still be seen in the area. The area has not been used as a firing range for over 60 years. (Then, PHPC via Tex Johnson; now, Philip Maechling.)

The target area photograph in the Pattee Canyon area was taken in 1936. Soldiers were concealed under the berm and after the final firing would put up a disc at each target to show the hit. The targets were placed in front of the berm, which is still intact but has mostly caved in. The now photograph shows remains of the wooden structure that the soldiers were concealed under, but all evidence of the target stands have disappeared. (Then, PHPC via Tex Johnson; now, Philip Maechling.)

This U.S. Forest Service (USFS) photograph is from 1935, a year after the original remains of Fort Fizzle were burned. Breastworks were erected in 1877 as a result of the Nez Perce Indians passing through the area on their way east. The army at Fort Missoula and citizens of Missoula were at this site to try and stop the Nez Perce, who simply went around the fort—thus the name Fort Fizzle. The original breastworks were where the present parking lot is now located several miles from Lolo on U.S. Highway 12. (Then, USFS, No. 313583; now, Philip Maechling.)

U.S. FOREST SERVICE AND THE CIVILIAN CONSERVATION CORPS

The U.S. Forest Service was established in 1905, and Missoula was designated as the first regional office. The service has been an economic and employment staple for the community ever since. Its area at one time extended from eastern Washington to the western Dakotas. In this 1920 photograph, fire equipment is being loaded at the Forest Service warehouse at 240 West Pine Street. This is now a parking lot for city hall. (USFS, No. 150162.)

The Nine Mile Civilian Conservation Corps (CCC) was established in 1933, and the camp was established 3 miles north of the Nine Mile Ranger Station west of Missoula. It continued in service until 1942 and at one time was the largest CCC camp in the nation. The buildings were removed during World War II, and some were sent up to Canada for construction of the new Alaska Highway. Remnants of the camp remain today, including foundations of the buildings. A replica of the entrance gate was constructed at its approximate original site as a Boy Scouts of America project. This photograph was taken in August 1941. (Then, USFS, No. 413859; now, Stan Cohen.)

This photograph showing the headquarters buildings was taken in 1933 by prominent photographer K. D. Swan of the USFS. Most of these buildings were prefab units built in 20-foot sections and put together to form a 20-foot-by-60-foot building. These were used for barracks, mess halls, recreation, and education facilities. Some of these buildings were taken to Hale Field for use by smokejumpers after the war. The only other visual remains of the camp are this large fireplace and chimney from the officers' quarters. (Then, USFS, No. 283496; now, Stan Cohen.)

The original radio station that the U.S. Forest Service used for years to coordinate calls from fire lookouts and ranger stations still stands at the top of Whitaker Drive in the South Hills area. It was used through the 1950s and now has been restored and is used as a community center owned by the Missoula Parks and Recreation Department. The original switchboard was still there in 1978, when a parks photographer was working in the building. (Then, USFS, No. 413887; now, Philip Maechling.)

U.S. FOREST SERVICE AND THE CIVILIAN CONSERVATION CORPS

The aerial fire depot and smokejumper base are located at the west end of the Missoula International Airport. The jump base was moved here in 1954 from the Nine Mile area, and the entire complex was dedicated by Pres. Dwight D. Eisenhower that year on September 22. It was the largest crowd in Montana up to that time. The base has been greatly expanded through the years, and several Forest Service facilities have been built to the west. The jump base is the largest in the nation. The tower shown is the parachute loft. (Then, USFS, No. 477421; now, Stan Cohen.)

Fire lookout towers such as this dotted the mountains around Missoula area since the 1930s, and a few are still standing. Some are still used in the summer, and some are used as recreation sites. Most fire patrolling in the forests is now conducted by aerial surveys. This type of structure was designated as an L-4 design in the 1930s by Clyde Fickes. It was prefabricated and was usually hauled by horse or mule to its remote location. Three of these lookouts are on display in Missoula. This one is at the Historical Museum at Fort Missoula, one is at the new Museum of Forest Service History, and one is indoors at the U.S. Forest Service Visitor's Center. (Then, USFS, No. 365178; now Stan Cohen.)

UNIVERSITY OF MONTANA

Campbell Field was located at the corner of South Higgins Avenue and South Avenue. It was built after World War II and named for John T. Campbell, a prominent lawyer in Missoula. It was home to the university's baseball team at one time and also home to the pro baseball team the Timberjacks from the 1950s. The present Missoula Osprey team continues the legacy of the Timberjacks. The field was torn down in 1968, and the university's football stadium was moved to this site until the present Washington-Grizzly Stadium was completed in 1986. The area now contains the university's soccer and track facilities. This photograph was probably taken in the 1950s. (PHPC.)

One of the most prominent symbols of Missoula and the university is the *M* on Mount Sentinel, which is owned by the university. Forestry students were responsible for cutting the first trail up to the site, and by 1909 the *M* was outlined by rocks first whitewashed by the junior class. In 1912, the freshman class built a wooden *M*, but it was destroyed by a windstorm in 1915, and that year the class built a stone *M* in its place. Every year, the freshman class carried on the traditions of whitewashing the *M* until the present *M* was constructed of concrete in 1968. Today the trail up to the *M* is widely used by university students and Missoula citizens for physical exercise. (Then, PHPC; now, Ross Carlson.)

The University of Montana campus has only four buildings in this 1903 image: University Hall, Women's Hall, the Men's Gymnasium with the athletic field behind it, and Science Hall. The town of Missoula is in the far distance. The long lines of trees were planted on Arbor Day, 1896. The neighborhoods south of the Clark Fork River are nearly empty east of Higgins Avenue; neighborhood development did not begin in earnest until the streetcar line to Higgins Avenue was completed in 1912. Development west of Higgins Avenue on the east-west streets is visible. The university campus has grown physically and added many thousands of students in over 100 years. University Hall, with its distinctive clock tower, remains, as does Women's Hall (now the Mathematics Building). The Men's Gymnasium was torn down in 1965; Science Hall (then known as the Venture Center) followed in 1983, replaced by the Davidson Honors College in 1996. Geographically, economically, and socially, the university is irrevocably part of Missoula. (Then, UM, No. A III a-40, Morton J. Elrod Photographs, K. Ross Toole Archives; now, photograph by Chris Autio.)

This wide-angle view appears to have been taken in 1922, the year of construction of the heating plant in the center and the completion of the new library, now the Social Sciences Building, in the upper left. The home in the lower left is the Prescott House, built in 1888 by Clarence Prescott, a nephew of C. P. Higgins. His son Clarence lived in the house until his death in 1993, and the house was saved and restored by a donation from Phyllis Washington. It is now used for university functions and weddings. Today this entire area is filled with university buildings. The student population is now over 14,000. (Then, PHPC; now Ross Carlson.)

The majestic Main or University Hall is the oldest remaining building on the university's campus. It was designed by A. J. Gibson, construction started in 1898, and the building opened in 1899. In its first years, it housed classrooms, an auditorium, a gym, labs, the library, a museum, and offices. This view was taken in the early 1900s. Gibson would design the first five buildings on campus. Next door was the Science Hall, the first building completed on campus. It was torn down in 1983, and the Davidson Honors College building now occupies the site. Main Hall's interior has been modified through the years, and it now serves as offices for the university's administrative staff. Its roof has recently been redone. In 1953, the Memorial Carillon, with 47 bells, was installed in the 122-foot bell tower. A clock is also in the tower. (Then, PHPC; now, Philip Maechling.)

The campus had greatly increased in this late 1920s view. Main Hall is the central building with the football field behind it. Several buildings to the lower left were constructed during World War I to house student officers. The Forestry Building, North Hall, Men's Gym, law school, library, Science Hall, and Natural Sciences Buildings were completed. The Math Building, formally the women's dorm and the third building on campus, is to the far left. The oval was still open to vehicles, and the area from the university towards the river was just beginning to fill in. (Then, PHPC; now, Ross Carlson.)

This is an early-1900s view of part of the oval and the area to the west. For years, the oval was open to horse-drawn wagons and carriages and later on to vehicles. The large house at the left edge of the oval was home to the university's president. The present University Avenue was open up to the edge of the oval. Through the years, many large and elegant homes were built in this open area that is now known as the University District. The university is in the process of replanting trees that once lined the oval. (Then, PHPC; now, Ross Carlson.)

The original women's dormitory building was designed by A. J. Gibson and completed in 1904. Now known as the Math Building, it originally had major porch entries on the east, west, and north facades and a small kitchen wing on the south side. Recently the university added onto the building to make it more accessible to all, for which it was awarded a historic preservation award by the Missoula Historic Preservation Commission. (Then, UM; now, Philip Maechling.)

TRANSPORTATION

This photograph shows part of the Western Montana Fairgrounds and Hale Field in 1939. The first fair was held in 1879, and it was moved to this site in 1915. The building at the bottom was constructed by the WPA in the 1930s and is still in use. The two horse barns burned down in 1966, and horse racing ended in 2007. Hale Field, Missoula's first official airport, was established in 1927 and was named for county surveyor Dick Hale. It was mainly used by Johnson Flying Service until the service moved to the present airport in 1954 and the site became the home of University of Montana College of Technology and Sentinel High School. Today the fair is still the highlight of the summer season in the county. (USFS.)

In 1941, the present airport west of Missoula was opened as a WPA project. Northwest Airlines was the first commercial airline to service Missoula. A small terminal was built and expanded through the years. This photograph is from the 1960s, and the terminal has gone through several additions since then. The tower is still in use, but a new, taller one will be built in 2010. The entire airport, which actually has three names—Johnson-Bell Airport, Missoula County Airport, and Missoula International Airport—is now served by four airlines, two flight base operators, the largest aerial firefighting company in the country, an aviation museum, and other aviation facilities. The U.S. Forest Service has its aerial firefighting services at the west end of the airport. (Then, PHPC; now, Stan Cohen.)

The Marent Gulch Trestle, built in 1883 by the Northern Pacific Railway at the base of Evaro Hill northwest of Missoula, was 226 feet high and 668 feet long. It was the highest wooden trestle railroad bridge in the world at the time. The railway was completed in 1883. This view is from 1885, when the trestle was being replaced with steel supports. Both the wooden and steel supports can be seen. The trestle has been in use ever since, now by Montana Raillink. A major military collector and dealer now owns the property at the base of the trestle. (Then, PHPC; now, Stan Cohen.)

The Northern Pacific Railway (NP) reached Missoula in 1883. A wooden depot was constructed at the end of Higgins Avenue but became controversial when it cut off access from the north side of Missoula to the downtown area. It was destroyed by an arson fire in 1896, and this Renaissance Revival–style building was constructed in its place, opening in 1901. It served the community until passenger service was discontinued in 1978. The building has been used as a brewery, bar, and restaurant and is now office space. The area, known as Circle Square, is now the site of the popular farmers' market and a 1902 NP steam engine. (Then, Washington State Historical Society; now, Philip Maechling.)

TRANSPORTATION

This bird's-eye view of the Northern Pacific rail yards, just north of the downtown area, was taken by NP photographer F. Jay Haynes in 1894. The roundhouse can just be seen to the extreme right. The first wooden depot burned down in 1896, and construction on the present depot had not yet started. The railway opened up trade and commerce between the East and West when the railroad was completed in 1883, and Missoula expanded considerably thereafter. (Then, MHS, No. H-304; now, Philip Maechling.)

Almost 50 years later, the rail yard and the area around it have greatly expanded. The roundhouse complex is in the foreground, and the present depot is in the middle of the photograph. The courthouse is to the extreme left, St. Francis Catholic Church is in the middle, and the Scared Heart Academy is just to the right. Many hotels were built close to the rail yard in this period but are mostly gone now. The large white building to the west of the depot is now the Depot Restaurant. All the rail facilities are gone except for the turntable. (Then, Library of Congress; now, Philip Maechling.)

The Milwaukee Road's elegant station on Missoula's south side was opened in 1910. The tall tower was added so that it could be seen from the Northern Pacific depot at the north end of Higgins Avenue. The station served the community until 1980, although passenger service ended in 1961. The line was electrified from Harlowton, Montana, to Avery, Idaho, in 1916. After 1980, the depot went through several owners, including a restaurant on the first floor. Today there are some offices in the building, but most of the area is taken up by the national office of the Boone and Crockett Club. (Then, PHPC; now, Philip Maechling.)

One of the original electrical substations built along the route of the Milwaukee Road in 1915 is still standing at Primrose just off Mullan Road west of Missoula. These were built about every 40 miles to provide electric power for the railroad. All of the original electrical equipment was removed from this station in the 1970s, and the brick building has been used off and on for storage ever since. (Then, Bill and Jan Taylor; now, Stan Cohen.)

AROUND TOWN

In this logging setup in the Lolo Forest near Missoula, a log chain slide system runs along the ground to get logs to a loading site. Timber was the main staple of industry in the Missoula area for over 100 years but has now practically disappeared. No sawmills are left in the area, but a large pulp mill operated until 2010 in the Frenchtown area. This is now in the Rattlesnake National Recreation Area and has been mostly grown over since this photograph was taken close to 100 years ago. (USFS, No. 173174.)

This photograph was taken looking northwest from the top of the Palace Hotel about 1920. The Missoula County Courthouse, designed by Missoula architect A. J. Gibson and completed in 1910, is surrounded by single- and multifamily residences, with few businesses. Visible to the left are St. Francis Xavier Church, Loyola High School, and Sacred Heart Academy. St. Patrick's Hospital is to the left, out of the photograph. Much changed by a 1966 addition, but the original portions of the courthouse have been restored. Most of the housing structures in the area are now businesses and offices. The Lenox Hotel was restored as affordable housing in 2000. Sacred Heart Academy was demolished in 1979, when it merged with Loyola High School and moved to Edith Street. St. Francis and its associated Catholic Block buildings remain, but their future is in question. St. Patrick Hospital has expanded considerably, responding to the growing medical needs of western Montana, with a new hospital in 1984 and the Broadway Building in 2000. (Then, UM, No. 94-1556, R. H. McKay Photographs, K. Ross Toole Archives; now photograph by Marcy James.)

The original Missoula County Courthouse and jail was built in 1870. In 1889, a separate brick jail was erected just to the west. At this time, the county encompassed most of western Montana, with several counties created from it in the early 1900s. This building was moved to the north side when the new courthouse opened in 1910. For years, the building was split into apartments, but it has been vacant for years and needs complete restoration. (Then, UM, No. 77-247; now, Philip Maechling.)

Members of the Veterans of Foreign Wars (VFW) stand at attention by the doughboy statue on the southeast corner of the courthouse in 1927. The VFW began in 1899 and is still in existence. This type of statue was placed in many cities across the country to honor World War I veterans. Plaques are placed on the statue for county soldiers killed in both World War I and II. This statue was erected on the courthouse lawn in 1927. The present-day veterans are members of the local American Legion color guard. (Then, PHPC; now, Philip Maechling.)

Old Hellgate Village was established in 1860 along the original Mullan Road, about 4 miles west of downtown Missoula. The first store was opened by Frank Worden and C. P. Higgins as a trading post for traders, miners, and Native Americans traveling through the area. In 1864, a mill was built in what is now downtown Missoula next to the Clark Fork River, and the new town of Missoula Mills built out from there. Road agents were tried and hung nearby by vigilantes at the original store site. This view is from 1947, when a few buildings were still standing. Nothing remains of this site today, and it has been a trailer court for many years. (Then, UM, No. 87-282; now, Philip Maechling.)

The south bank of the Clark Fork River is pictured about 1890. According to Salish elder Louis Adams, these canvas teepees were the temporary homes of Salish who came to Missoula to harvest bitterroot, which at one time was abundant throughout the valley and the surrounding hills. Salish harvesting this staple root was a common sight in Missoula until the 1960s, when development of the prime growing areas and changes in native lifestyles altered this. The area went from food source to transportation center when it became the Missoula rail yard for the Milwaukee, Chicago, and St. Paul Railroad, completed in 1908. The railroad went bankrupt in 1980 and removed the rail yard. Now the area is home to popular walking and bicycling trail, athletic fields, and a small piece of restored prairie where the tiny bitterroot flowers bloom every spring. (Then, UM, No. 72-12, attributed to Charles Wadsworth Lombard, K. Ross Toole Archives; now, photograph by Marcy James.)

This never-before-published photograph shows a large building at the present site of the parking garage at the corner of Ryman and Main Streets. The second floor of the building housed the local Fraternal Order of Moose, with different branches of the order posing in the street in 1947. There was a roller rink on the top floor, and Ormesher Grocery occupied the first floor. On December 30, 1951, the building caught fire, and for 10 hours the fire department fought not only the fire but also the very cold temperatures. The front wall eventually collapsed, and three firemen—Bernard J. Albright, Walter E. Cain, and Edward Sayler—died. After the fire, new structures were built until the new city parking garage was opened in November 1993. (Then, Dennis Sain Photo; now, Philip Maechling.)

This building at the corner of Higgins Avenue and Broadway was completed in 1911 and housed the Western Montana National Bank. It still is one of the most prominent buildings in the downtown area. On April 11, 1911, ex-president Theodore Roosevelt spoke from a platform at the building's corner during his last presidential campaign. Years later, the building was converted to street-level retail and condominium offices on the upper floors. It is now called the Montana Building, and there are plans to restore the facade back to its original look as much as possible. The historic photograph was taken in the 1920s. (Then, PHPC; now, Philip Maechling.)

AROUND TOWN

This view of Mount Jumbo on Wednesday, August 24, 1910, is very important, as it shows the snow line of a summer storm at about the 4,000-foot elevation. This date is early for snow, but it came at a very opportune time. It helped put out the disastrous fires that blew up a few days earlier along the Idaho-Montana border to the west and burned over 3 million acres; it was thereafter called the "Big Burn." Eighty-five people were killed at various locations in Idaho. Refugees poured into Missoula on both railroads from the west, especially when part of the town of Wallace, Idaho, burned down. (Then, PHPC; now, Philip Maechling.)

The Babs Apartments at 120 South Fourth Street West opened in 1905 as the Garden City Business College. It was designed by A. J. Gibson in a Queen Anne commercial mode and was later converted into apartments. In 2008, the apartment building, which was run down, was remodeled into condominiums. (Then, PHPC; now, Philip Maechling.)

This site at the corner of South Higgins Avenue and South Fifth Street West has gone from a gas station to an ice cream parlor. This is a McKay photograph taken in the late 1920s. The top of the Babs Apartments can be seen from the top of the adjoining building. At some point in time, the corner was converted to retail outlets, and in 1996 the Big Dipper Ice Cream Store opened. (Then, PHPC; now, Philip Maechling.)

The Elks Club (BPOE No. 383) at the corner of Pattee and Front Streets was designed by Link and Haire and erected in 1910. For many years, the bottom floor was used by the nearby Missoula Mercantile to display wagons and implements for sale. Lodge No. 383 was established in Missoula in 1897, and the entire building is still in use by the lodge, with a bar and dining facilities on the first floor and meeting rooms and apartments on the upper floors. At one time, there was a gym in the basement. (Then, PHPC; now, Philip Maechling.)

AROUND TOWN

Missoula's art museum is located in the old 1903 Carnegie Library on Pattee Street. Built with Carnegie money and designed by A. J. Gibson, it was only one floor. In 1913, a second floor was added, designed by Ole Bakke. A new library was built on East Front Street in 1974, and the Missoula Art Museum took over the building. In 2007, the original building was remodeled, mainly inside, and a new modern addition was built on the south side. (Then, PHPC; now, Philip Maechling.)

The First National Bank Building was constructed in 1891 and is the oldest continuously open bank in the state. This building stood at the corner of South Higgins Avenue and Front Street until demolished in 1962. The building also housed the Flathead Reservation Information Agency, a real estate firm, and a wallpaper store. On the right is the original Missoula mill, which was torn down in 1912. Western Union was on the Front Street side, and the Star Theater and a wine shop were in the adjacent building. In November 2009, a new six-story building replaced the 1962 building. The bank is now called the First Interstate Bank. (Then, PHPC; now, Philip Maechling.)

Missoula's oldest major downtown building is the impressive Higgins Block, built by Missoula pioneer C. P. Higgins in 1889 for his Western Montana National Bank. Unfortunately he died the same year. The Higgins house was at the extreme right, where a small addition was built in 1911. The north part of the building, facing Higgins Avenue, was the first site for the D. J. Hennessy Mercantile Company. This historic photograph was taken in the early 1900s, after the store moved out. During World War II, the front facade was altered with horizontal picture windows, but it was restored to the original look in the 1980s. The building is now owned by the Sterling Savings Bank, and the upper floors have been restored to their original look and rented out for professional offices and art galleries. (Then, PHPC; now, Philip Maechling.)

The second-oldest complete building in the downtown area is the 1890–1891 Missoula Hotel. The former three-story hotel is located at the corner of Main and Ryman Streets. It is built on a massive granite base but has been altered several times in its history, including by fire. At one time, there was a popular restaurant and nightclub in the basement. In the 1950s, the building was converted to apartments, with retail outlets and a clock repair shop on the ground floor. (Then, PHPC; now, Philip Maechling.)

This complete view of the Missoula Mercantile building was taken by R. H. McKay in 1927. The building has stayed largely intact through the years, except that the upper windows on the Higgins Avenue side have been filled in. The business was known as Eddy, Hammond, and Company in 1876, and the first part of the building, the southeast corner, was constructed in 1877. With additions through the years, it was known as the Missoula Mercantile, then the Bon Marche, and finally was last owned by the Macy's chain. Macy's closed in 2010. (Then, PHPC; now, Philip Maechling.)

The third Florence Hotel is pictured as it appeared after it opened in 1942. The first hotel on site, built in 1888, burned down in 1913. The rebuilt hotel on site burned down in 1936. The present building was constructed by the Missoula Real Estate Association for $600,000. It had 175 rooms, a main dining room, a coffee shop, a cocktail lounge, banquet rooms, and retail outlets. It was billed as "America's Finest Small Hotel" and was the social center of the city. The art moderne–style building closed in the 1970s and was turned into office space. It is now owned by ALPS, Inc., and the elegant lobby area has been restored with a restaurant adjacent to the lobby. The Kohn Jewelry clock has been restored and still stands elegantly on the sidewalk. (Then, PHPC; now, Philip Maechling.)

One of Missoula's most prominent historical downtown buildings is the Wilma Theater, first called the Smead-Simons Building, which opened in 1921. It has gone through several owners and is still undergoing restoration. It was named the Wilma after builder W. A. Simons's wife. At one time, there was a swimming pool in the basement, and a restaurant now occupies part of the space. A replica of the large outside sign was placed back on the building in 2008. The building is still used for movies and other theatrical events, and the former apartments have all been converted to condominiums. The two buildings to the right were both destroyed by fire in 1932 and 1936. (Then, PHPC; now, Philip Maechling.)

A 1920s view of the Labor Temple on East Main Street was also the home of the local Dodge car dealership, Murphy Motors. The building was constructed in 1916–1917 and still serves as headquarters for various local unions, with a bar on the first floor. The painted sign on the side of the building can still be seen, and a small building previously used as a gas station is still standing on the lot next door. Missoula has had snow this deep, but it is not as frequent of an occurrence as in the past. (Then, PHPC; now, Philip Maechling.)

AROUND TOWN

This McKay photograph is of the new H. O. Bell Ford dealership at the corner of South Higgins Avenue and South Fourth Street about 1929. Bell came to Missoula and bought the Ford dealership in 1915. He and Bob Johnson were very active in local aviation, and the airport is named Johnson-Bell Field. The building behind the large one is still in use, but the main building was torn down in the early 1990s to make room for a gas and convenience store. Bell died in 1971. (Then, PHPC; now, Philip Maechling.)

The H. O. Bell home, at 380 Keith Avenue in Missoula's University District, is pictured about 1925. Bell came to Missoula in 1915 and bought the Ford automobile dealership. He built his home in 1921. In 1929, he opened H. O. Bell Company at the corner of South Higgins Avenue and South Fourth Street and became an important businessman. Highly interested in aviation, Bell served as chair of the Missoula County Airport Board for over 30 years. The Missoula International Airport, formerly known as Johnson-Bell Field, was named for him. He died in 1971. By 1951, the homes surrounding this one were all present. Now the University Area Historic District and other historic Missoula neighborhoods face issues of preserving or changing historic structures, density rates, and razing homes to replace them with larger ones. (Then, UM, No. 94-1417, R. H. McKay Photographs, K. Ross Toole Archives; now, photograph by Kristi Hager.)

The Bonner mansion, at Gerald and Connell Streets in the University District, is pictured in June 1928. Edward Bonner came to Missoula in 1866 and established Bonner and Welch, later the Missoula Mercantile Company. His business supplied the Northern Pacific Railroad with lumber. In 1891, he built this elegant home, which occupied the entire block. He and his wife, Carrie, had two daughters, Lenita and Bessie. Lenita married Edward Spotswood, a physician and surgeon, and the house became theirs; they had two children, Edward Jr. and Lenita. Lenita Spotswood last lived in the Bonner mansion in 1959. The City of Missoula had an opportunity to buy the mansion for $100,000; when it did not, the home was razed. The Connell Apartments, Lynwood Condominiums, and Spotswood Apartments now occupy the block. The photographer found young men on the balconies playing guitars on an Indian summer day. (Then, UM, No. 94-1408, R. H. McKay Photographs, K. Ross Toole Archives; now, photograph by Kristi Hager, 2006.)

The Rattlesnake Valley is seen from Mount
Sentinel between 1891 and 1894. The valley
is lightly populated, with a few working-class
and railroad workers' homes. In the foreground
are the riverside farms that became the Hughes
Gardens in 1909 and gave Missoula its "Garden
City" name. Just up the valley are Thomas
Greenough's piles of wood. He cut pine and
tamarack trees from the valley and sold them to
the railroads and mines, making himself one of
Missoula's wealthiest men. He built a mansion
nearby in 1897. The changes in the Rattlesnake
Valley in more than 110 years are visible through
thicker trees on Mount Sentinel. Hughes
Gardens supplied Missoulians with produce until
1971, when the land was sold to the Gateway
Corporation for commercial development along
East Broadway. Interstate 90 cut across this
landscape in 1966, making it necessary to move
Greenough's mansion and demolish many other
buildings. The residential neighborhood continues
to develop and change, with a variety of housing
stock and resident demographics. (Then, UM,
No. 75-72, Chauncey Woodworth Photographs,
K. Ross Toole Archives; now, photograph by
Chris Autio, 2006.)

On January 1, 1942, a disastrous fire burned the Ross Block at the corner of Higgins Avenue and Pine Street downtown. Yandt's Men's Wear was gutted, and the next-door Hotel Shapard building, constructed in 1909, was destroyed with a loss of $350,000. Temperatures never got above 15 degrees below zero. Yandt's rebuilt and stayed in business for years as one of the city's finest men's store. (Then, Doug Hacker photograph; now, Philip Maechling.)

This dramatic photograph shows the 1889 Hammond Building at the corner of Higgins Avenue and Main Street on fire on October 9, 1932. The building was constructed by prominent city businessman A. B. Hammond. Due to the Depression, only a one-floor building could be financed as a replacement on the site in 1933–1934. The Wilma Theater is to the left, and the First National Bank is across the street. The Missoula Drug Company was a fixture in the old building for many years. The fire truck is possibly the 1918 American LaFrance engine that will be on display at the Historical Museum at Fort Missoula in 2010. (Then, PHPC; now, Philip Maechling.)

This view of downtown was taken from an aircraft in the 1940s after construction of the third Florence Hotel building. Significantly, a number of buildings in this image still exist, including the Mercantile, Higgins Block, Dixon Duncan Block, and Montana buildings. The current image was taken from the Florence Building. The North Hills and Hellgate Canyon still frame Missoula's downtown. (Then, PHPC/UM; now, Philip Maechling.)

Missoula's second building constructed just for a high school is the present Hellgate High School on South Higgins Avenue. Another Gibson design, it opened as Missoula County High School in November 1908 as the only public high school in the county. Now there are four public high schools and one Catholic high school in the county. Additions were built through the years as the population increased, but a fire in 1931 gutted the school, and a flat roof was added upon reconstruction. In 1965, the building was renamed Hellgate High School. (Then, UM; now, Philip Maechling.)

The old Roosevelt School on South Sixth Street was built in September 1904 as a four-year high school. The building was soon overcrowded and reverted to a grade school when the new high school was opened in 1908. It was named Roosevelt Grade School after Pres. Theodore Roosevelt. A new Roosevelt Grade School was opened in 1954 on Edith Street, and the old building became the administration offices for School District One, now Missoula County Public Schools. (Then, PHPC; now, Philip Maechling.)

Amalgamated Sugar Co. Plant - Missoula, Mont. - 46.

At one time, the Missoula area was a large producer of sugar beets. The American Crystal Sugar Company established a large factory just off present South Reserve Street in 1918 to process the beets into crystal sugar. This site was also the grounds for the Western Montana Fair until it was moved to its present site in 1915. The factory closed in 1966, and these two buildings are the last remnants of this major industrial complex. (Then, PHPC; now, Philip Maechling.)

The First Presbyterian Church was designed by A. J. Gibson, who was also member of the congregation. This English Gothic Revival church boasts a 62-foot-tall bell tower and handsome leaded-glass windows. The church is in the center of Missoula's Southside Historic District and has local values associated with it due to its first pastor, the Reverend John Maclean, who was the father of Norman Maclean, author of *A River Runs Through It* and *Young Men and Fire*. (Then, PHPC; now, Philip Maechling.)

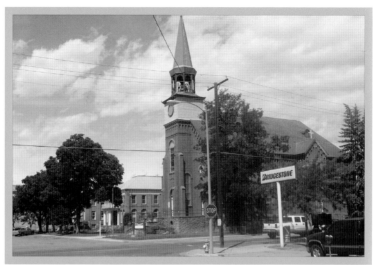

The Catholic Block was comprised of four significant historic buildings: St. Francis Xavier Church (1891–1892, National Register of Historic Places listing 1982), St. Francis Xavier Parish Rectory (1902–1909), Loyola High School for Catholic Boys (1912), and St. Frances Xavier School (1927, demolished in 2010). The St. Francis Xavier Catholic Church is a monumental Romanesque Revival–style building with a central tower rising to a height of 144 feet. These buildings are excellent cultural resources, having retained their original architectural character and use. As of this writing, the elementary school is scheduled for demolition. (Then, PHPC; now, Philip Maechling.)

This historic view of the Commercial Building at the Western Montana Fair is from the late 1950s. The fair was established in 1879 and moved to the present site in 1915, when this building was constructed. The fair was discontinued for several years during the Depression and in 1941 after a fire destroyed the grandstand and other buildings. Due to World War II, the fair was not started again until 1954, but it has continued ever since then. Since it contains a large area, it has been used for many other events through the years, and there have been many studies as to moving it to another site or upgrading the buildings and grounds. (Then, PHPC; now, Philip Maechling.)

The original Target Range School was built in 1893 as School District 23 on South Avenue and is the last lapboard-sided school in the Missoula Valley. The first students were children from troops stationed at nearby Fort Missoula. The *Target Range* name is associated with the firing range on the open field nearby Macauley Butte used by the military into the 1920s. This little schoolhouse went through several additions through the years, including the last in 1972 on the south side to house the girls' locker room. After the new school was built, this little building became a storage facility. A few years ago, its restoration became a Boy Scouts of America project to make it a center for community events. Unfortunately the project was temporarily halted in 2009. (Then, Kris Crawford; now, Philip Maechling.)

CHAPTER 7

AROUND
THE COUNTY

A popular recreation area is located 35 miles southwest of Missoula at Lolo Hot Springs. The hot springs were used by Native Americans for hundreds of years. The original hotel was built in 1903 and was used into the 1950s. Cabins were built along the granite outcrops but were later moved to the adjoining Granite Hot Springs. The first swimming pool opened in 1918. Today the springs are a very popular year-round recreation area with a bar, restaurant, swimming pool, motel, and camping area. (PHPC.)

Bonner, Montana, is pictured about 1945. The mill was founded in 1885 by the Montana Improvement Company to exploit the rich timber resources of the Blackfoot Valley. It includes the dam, planing mill, powerhouse, sawmill, sorting table, store, office, and bunkhouse—all surrounded by company housing. The two-story building in the foreground was Bonner's first school, built in 1889; it also served as the Masonic lodge and public hall. Open space behind the houses was a community garden from 1918 to the mid-1940s. Bonner's mill grew physically and thrived economically through ownership by the Anaconda Company and Champion International. The public hall was torn down in the 1940s, as was the grand Hotel Margaret, but many of the company-built houses remain largely unchanged. Peering through the trees, thick after 100 years of fire suppression, the photographer took this image standing on a pile of boards as dogs barked at him. Stimson Lumber Company closed the mill in 2008. (Then, UM, No. 57(IX):35, Anaconda Forest Products Company Records, K. Ross Toole Archives; now, photograph by Chris Autio.)

Bonita, Montana, is pictured around 1900. Bonita was about 25 miles east of Missoula near Bearmouth. It was established in the mid-1880s and, like hundreds of other settlements along transcontinental railroad lines, serviced the engines with fuel and water. It also had a steam-operated sawmill. About 100 people lived in and around Bonita, including railroad workers, farmers, ranchers, and businesspeople. This image shows nearby buildings with freight and telegraph offices; a luggage trolley is in the foreground. Bonita formally ended its existence in 1942, when the post office closed. None of the buildings in the earlier photograph exist today. The 1908 flood of the Clark Fork River washed away the original railroad tracks in the area; the railroad replaced them with double tracks soon after. With the help of local resident Renee Householder and an old map, the photographer found the likely location—where railroad ties now serve as fence posts on the very straight road created on the old railroad grade. (Then, UM, No. 77-104, K. Ross Toole Archives, Maureen and Mike Mansfield Library, gift of Tim Gordon; now, photograph by Kristi Hager.)

Camp Paxson consists of 20 log structures with a main lodge, 15 sleeping cabins, two bathhouses, a pump house, and a caretaker's house. It is the only Civilian Conservation Corps/Works Progress Administration (CCC/WPA)–constructed youth camp in the state of Montana. It began as a rustic camp in 1924 and was completed in its present condition in 1939–1940. It was designed to fit into a small peninsula on Seeley Lake, retaining all of its old-growth timber and natural integrity. It is now leased by the Missoula Children's Theater. (Then, PHPC; now, Philip Maechling.)

AROUND THE COUNTY

Stark School was built in 1915 between Butler and Kennedy Creeks to provide an education for the children of miners, loggers, and ranchers in the middle Nine Mile Valley. The school is one of just two remaining original buildings left from the community of Stark. Gold mining from the 1870s on caused the first boom in the Nine Mile Valley. The gold played out, and most of the small communities, like Old Town, Martina, and Stark, disappeared. At one time, there were hundreds of people in Stark, and it had a post office and an ice cream parlor. By 1916, the Anaconda Company had set up a very active lumber operation, and by 1926 the place was empty. The school closed in 1929. (Then, Carol Guthrie; now, Philip Maechling.)

The historic Nine Mile House was originally built across the road from the present bar and restaurant in 1893 as a two-story restaurant and dance hall. The upper Nine Mile Valley was a mining area, and a small mill was built at the lower end of the valley. George Brown and his family started and ran the business into the late 1930s. In 1947, the building was moved across the road and the top floor removed. The present building has been operated as a bar and restaurant ever since. (Then, PHPC; now, Philip Maechling.)

The historic Nine Mile Ranger Station and Remount Station was constructed by the CCC in 1935, and it has supplied mules for the Forest Service up to the present day. It is located up the Nine Mile Road a few miles off of Interstate 90, about 25 miles west of Missoula. The original remount station was established here in 1930. The mule string stationed here has been in parades all over the country as well as being used to pack supplies into the backcountry. A visitor's center is open in the summer. (Then, USFS; now, Philip Maechling.)

Traveler's Rest in Lolo is one of two National Historic Landmarks in Missoula County. The other is the Lolo/Nez Perce Trail, which goes through Traveler's Rest. Originally the site was mislocated approximately a mile east of the current site. Modern scientific investigation located this site as the original Native American crossroads camp where the Lewis and Clark Expedition camped for many days in 1805 and 1806. The site is now managed as a Montana state park. (Then, Library of Congress; now, Philip Maechling.)

Before 1908, the Clark Fork and Big Blackfoot Rivers converged at this site. In 1908, the Bonner Dam and powerhouse was completed by W. A. Clark, one of Butte's copper kings, on the Clark Fork River by his Missoula Light and Power Company to supply power to the mills at Bonner and the city of Missoula. Toxic material from mining and smelting in Butte and Anaconda continued to build up in the pond behind the dam for almost 100 years, and the area became a federal Superfund site. In 2008, the dam and powerhouse were demolished, allowing the two rivers to join together and flow freely for the first time in 100 years. Milltown, Bonner, and the bridges over the Blackfoot River can be seen in the background. (Then, PHPC; now, Philip Maechling.)

DISCOVER THOUSANDS OF LOCAL HISTORY BOOKS FEATURING MILLIONS OF VINTAGE IMAGES

Arcadia Publishing, the leading local history publisher in the United States, is committed to making history accessible and meaningful through publishing books that celebrate and preserve the heritage of America's people and places.

Find more books like this at
www.arcadiapublishing.com

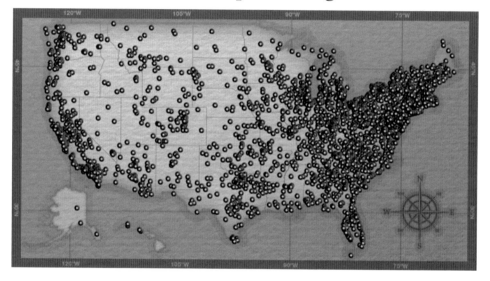

Search for your hometown history, your old stomping grounds, and even your favorite sports team.

Consistent with our mission to preserve history on a local level, this book was printed in South Carolina on American-made paper and manufactured entirely in the United States. Products carrying the accredited Forest Stewardship Council (FSC) label are printed on 100 percent FSC-certified paper.

MADE IN THE

USA